VICE AND VIRTUE

By: Malik Yasul Hasan Walker

THIS PAGE IS LEFT INTENTIALLY BLANK

TABLE OF CONTENTS

notes

PREFACE

"Virtues are as dangerous as vices, in so far as they are allowed to rule over one as authorities and laws coming from the outside, and not as qualities one develops one's self." - Friedrich Nietzsche

This book that I have written over the past four to five months has taken the shape of a cognitive behavioral therapy course (totally unintentionally). Firstly, I encountered the challenge of facing myself. In this encounter I started to notice numerous aspects of myself that I would never want to be perceived by me and/or any others. I allowed my flaws to be heard. In return I was given the ability to be completely genuine inwardly and outwardly.

Now I am like a free spirit able to live according to my own accord. This new ability has given me unfiltered and unbiased qualities needed to attack such an endeavor as creating cultures and establishing traditions from the root.

I will show why it is integral to focus on the development of our own vices and virtues. I will portray ways vices and virtues can be tools to be recognized and utilized every day. I will also explore this paradoxical world of morality expounding on ways virtues can be masks for deficiencies and how vices could help our efficiency to operate (good vices and bad virtues).

INTRODUCTION

I am a loser. Since the moment I have been able to make independent choices it seems as though I have not made one wholly holy decision. Ruled by bodily passions and other's opinions of my life, I have allowed my lifetime to be wasted. Ultimately, I have lost drive to be great and prove people wrong. I feel like I simply don't give a fuck anymore. My actions amount to nothing. I try so hard but receive nothing in return. This has brought me to the point of spilling my raw thoughts on to this page.

Chronic procrastinator and chronic masturbater is what I am now. The things I want to accomplish are always pushed to the back burner, and pursuit of money and bodily pleasures are brought to the forefront.

Unconsciously I have lost faith in myself and faith in God. I have always been afraid to admit but it seems true. I never tried as a child to do good and be great because it was that which came natural to me.

My faith in God was like the background force to my life that kept me going unconsciously. I prayed like it was second nature. My prayers were never self-indulged shit like they are now.

As a child I remember faithfully getting on my knees every night to pray for peace for the entire world. Not like my prayers now, all for myself. Justifiably maybe, I do need Higher assistance maybe as much as the world needs it. I do not know the moment this change occurred, but it is something I have noticed. Maybe this happened when my great grandmother Ola passed away and entered heaven. This is around the same time many drastic changes begin to take place in my life. For instance, like being evicted by "family" and/or doing many questionable things I know my child version would be ashamed of.

I became accustomed to mediocrity and I was okay with it. Doing things, I never thought I would do made me question myself. The only thing that remained the same was me being alive.

But the content of my character had been completely altered since a child. I was evolved as a kid, but it seemed I had devolved as I grew older. Now I have to read a thousand books to figure out who I am. But as a kid I knew who I am or grammatically correct who I was. Who I am naturally has always been loving and pure. But due to external influence I lost my way.

I always knew I was different in comparison to my peers. For instance, as a child all my peers were concerned with getting tattoos, having sex with girls and doing drugs. I lost my way when I started to compare who I was with others. I thought that to be different would mean that I was missing out on all the fun. I begin to be just like my peers, chasing women and giving a fuck about things I truly did not.

I was weak enough to allow external shit to break through to my character and who I was. I wanted to be liked and a cool guy. This hindered my natural growth of whatever I was becoming. As a kid I did not cuss, or did I view women as objects until the influence of others. I always knew these things were available to me, but I never gravitated towards any of these things. Instead I would turn away from fallacy and not give it the time of day. I have become scared to stand alone in my truth of who I am.

I know that it is easy to be true to yourself by yourself but to do you amongst others takes courage and fortitude. Most people are concerned with being liked and fitting in, instead of standing out. To stand out is lonely (is lonely indeed), but you will make friends based on people seeing you are not afraid to be alone. Fortitude is needed because people will try to tell you that your wrong for being you and not like them. Society has its standards and to go against all that shit will make you an outcast amongst a bunch of followers and cowards.

Courage is the enemy of cowardice behavior. Courage is necessary because it may be uncharted territory that no one you know has embarked upon. I noticed that when you are a different person (an individual) that others are not accustomed to, you will automatically stand out. To laugh while everyone else's frowns will make people wonder "why is he smiling?".

I remember as a child in elementary school, while in our schoolyard before the start of the school day, a classmate asks me why I was smiling? It was so abnormal to smile amongst a bunch of sad folks. I have learned also that to be your genuine self-amongst artificial people could make you view your behaviors as wrong. Fuck that shit! We need to be comfortable at all times being who we are. Even if someone seems to question that.

If I feel how I feel, no one should have the ability to influence that especially if I do not want them to. I do not allow someone's feelings to dictate how I feel internally. I do not care if the sky is falling down. If I feel content internally and I feel like smiling, no one will change that. It is not that I am happy about the sky falling. I just find insight when I look within. Others may allow external influences the opportunity to dictate how they feel within. But I know that greatness comes when you look with in and dig down deep to sustain your well-being. I am different because it is things I see and/or feel that others may not. Does that make me better? NO! But it does mean that I see something that others may deem invisible. To be laughed at or ridiculed does not feel good. I do not think it will ever feel pleasant. But it feels even worst to be just like everyone else.

CHAPTER ONE:

CONNECTING THE DOTS

Do you remember the activities from our childhood that had numbered dots? When once connected properly formed a detailed picture? This is basically what my life is now. I am in the process of reconnecting past moments that played key roles in my development. Figuring out where I must have connected the wrong dots to form a distorted picture. Somewhere along the way I got lost or perhaps distracted from point A to point B. Thinking back to times as a child, my life was all virtues and no vice. As a kid I was completely pure until age 13.

Prior to my 14th birthday, I never cursed or masturbated, which are two of my current vices (my list of vices is terribly long). I remember the moment the changes occurred. It was when I entered high school, I felt the need to make changes to be accepted. I stopped doing things that made me happy to adapt to new situations. I was skateboarding every day prior to my 14th birthday. I would go outside and do what I enjoyed despite what anyone said.

I replaced one virtue with a vice. For instance, skateboarding was replaced with craving for attention from women. Each virtue was replaced with a vice. Writing and other artistic endeavors were replaced with weed and masturbation. I am now 25 years old, and I am only now freeing myself from the grips of these vices. An entire decade has passed with my priorities being misdirected. This is something that makes me sad when I think about it. I think about my child version of myself and I wonder what he would think of me now? I had great aspirations as a child, which turned into me just getting high watching time go by for an entire decade. If I had not caught myself, I would have willingly destroyed my entire life without second thinking. I was deaf to advice and what others had to say even if it was beneficial. I learned that my pride would not mind if I fucked up my entire life, as long as I lived according to my own terms. Pride is a killer. But I only know what is right for me and I could only change when the time was meant for it. Not according to when someone else deemed necessary. I have hit rock bottom many times. I just dusted myself off and continued doing what I thought was right even when I was in the wrong.

CHAPTER TWO:

MOVING ON A WHIM

Moving on a whim is to make sudden decisions that some may consider irrational. These decisions are solely based upon knowledge acquired by yourself despite what others may think.

To move on a whim takes confidence and carelessness to a certain extent. You will see that it is best to internalize issues rather than externalization. People tend to assume something is wrong when you express problems openly. They tend to become sympathetic towards your troubles. Then proceeds them constantly asking if you are ok, as if you have a life ending problem. Personally, these pitiful behaviors annoy me very much. But this only happens when you allow issues to surface rather than solving internally.

It is best to be cheerful despite what you may be going through internally. I am aware of the constant dread that accompanies life. But ultimately, we must be grateful for our share of suffering because it is there for our refinement. This gratefulness will lead to the release of tension within and a healthy outlook will follow. Despite the spite cheerfulness is key!

CHAPTER THREE:

VIRTUE

Virtue has taught me who I am at my best moments in time. While vice has taught me who I am at my worst moments in time. Both has been significant learning tools for development. I cannot say which has been most beneficial because both has helped me significantly in many aspects. To lean towards vice or virtue solely is ineffective. Finding a mutual balance between vice and virtue will allow you to enter the realm of non-duality or amorality. Some virtues that I have utilized in my life has been patience, cheerfulness and great sleep. Patience has taught me how to endure. This stamina is needed for the rollercoaster of joys and sorrows that accompanies life. Patience has given me a natural calmness that has possessed my spirit. No longer am I anxiously waiting for what is next or dwelling on the past.

I am now in a calm state of equilibrium due to exercising patience. Patience has also given me the ability to control my impulsive behaviors. To not always feel the need to react based upon momentary feelings has set me apart from hot headed reactive individuals.

Cheerfulness has given me a light spirit, light heart and light mind. The ways and/or woes of the world can make one feel downtrodden and undermined. But cheerfulness lifts this weight off ones shoulders and allows flight over people who cannot seem to levitate due to stress weighing them down like lead.

Cheerfulness leads naturally to the third virtue that I consciously utilize in my life. Sleeping well is a virtue that some may not be privy to naturally. This is mainly due to stress and unsettled thoughts in the mind. A good night's sleep is a virtue that goes a long way in assisting you. Sleep has many benefits, such as giving one great energy and insightful dreams.

The term "virtue" originates from its Latin root "virtus". If virtue is rooted and sourced in its original form its meaning completely alters from its contemporary form. The original form of virtue was not primarily focused on goodness, piety and sainthood. "Virtus" in its original configuration meant virility, moral perfection, manhood, firmness, bravery and strength. As you can see from the definitions above that "virtue" deviated from its original form "virtus" over time and sadly completely lost its original connotations.

CHAPTER FOUR:

VICE

Vices are viewed as bad habits, but I dare to redefine them as our redeeming qualities and aspects that needs refocusing. To acknowledge your vices is very noble and it is a path for the perfection of humans. Some of my redeeming qualities are addictions, emotional attachments and anger (to keep the list short here). Addiction and emotional attachments stem from similar vices. But addiction always begins as something you enjoy then turns into a "crutch" of dependency then turns into something that eventually degrades you. This is the sequence of addiction. Learning to strengthen oneself from dependence of addictions will give one room for good addictions instead of degradations. Filling a void that only appears due to your feelings of lack will be replaced with whole, completeness and fullness. Solitude is to be able to live with yourself without external stimuli. Addictions have many forms. To name a few forms of addiction; sex, drugs, friends, pursuit of women, pursuit of money and pursuit of being a person who is liked are examples of addictions. Addiction comes from emotional attachments. Emotional attachments are things you may grow fond of to the point where you cannot see living without. This only causes you to have an inability to be able to deal with things like stress with your natural given utilities. A cure for emotional attachments and addictions alike will be you attempting to live without the things you once loved.

CHAPTER FIVE:

CORE

STRENGTHENING

When you develop integral parts of your mind, I call this core strengthening. You will strengthen your mind through solitude, meditation and gaining knowledge. To rid yourself of any weaknesses in the mind, you will need to be completely honest with traits you are unconscious of which maybe traits you do not want to consider about yourself. In modern psychology this is called "shadow work" coined by Carl Jung. In my opinion anger is the best vice to have. It is not something to get rid of, but rather something that must be recognized, controlled and redirected.

Many things people value in life causes one to have built up animosity. This animosity is not good for internal organs and could lead one to horrible disease. To control anger, you will have to acknowledge (with honesty) things you should and should not care about. Secondly, you will have to be able to let go of anything you deem unworthy of your anger. Then you will naturally prioritize your life to not have your energy misdirected. Vices are redeeming qualities and qualities that needs refocusing.

This core strengthening is full of rigorous exercises that you will face as challenges head on. An example of these challenges is to make an important conscious enactment of becoming. This becoming is your greater self or your ideal personality type. This should be something you consciously practice as a daily routine. This second self (or greater self) is to be modelled after the greatest of the present and the past.

Therefore, you must learn about the lives of all those who personified greatness. This second self is meant for you to embody all those qualities which makes humans great. Then you will naturally begin to embody this greater self because of the absorption of knowledge. You must identify as your greater self by not performing past behaviors.

CHAPTER SIX:

BEING RIGHTEOUS VERSUS BEING PRENTENTIOUS

Live as honest as possible to avoid just trying to be nice. Put yourself out there without changing who you are to cater to other unauthentic people. Honesty will make you a rare individual. Being real with yourself is more important than being real with others. Both are significant when you are becoming who you are.

But authenticity with yourself outweighs outward realness. People may not deserve your utmost authenticity, but you should try to be authentic as possible, perhaps with a filter when dealing with others. But if you hurt feelings or destroy relationships so be it because it is probably best that way!

People enjoy your unauthentic self because they will deem you more likable perhaps. But being nice is overrated while being authentic is under-utilized and underrated. Some will become accustomed to you coming out into the world with a mask. But wearing a mask around others all the time is a disservice to your true self, who deserves to see the light of day sometimes.

CHAPTER SEVEN:

SENSATIONS

"Sensations are to be recognized as ingredients of the free will"-Friedrich Nietzsche

Sensations are a byproduct of who you truly are. This is why it is terrible to hide what you may feel about yourself and the world around you. Shadow work is to *recognize* those flaws that are pushed away and *reconcile* anything that may be disturbing. To integrate yourself with hidden parts of yourself, will develop you into greatness.

As kids we never hide what we are. But as we grow into the world, we push things to the back burner to be more likable due to being threatened by the outside world. You have an urge to be awesome. Bring these qualities into reality by embodying every characteristic that you view as awesome. People will notice that you act different, walk different even talk different. Authenticity offers you the ability to become familiar with your sensations. Simply by knowing what you have propensities for, you become an individual. Authenticity is rare in society. Humanity follows status quo even when it is not something they wholeheartedly agree with. Society is synonymous with the herd. Status quo is existing trends upheld by the masses.

The superior humans will not align with the hype of the status quo, due to his personal principles which supersedes it. Just because one million people may adhere to an idea that does not make your idea any less valid in comparison. This goal will be to be a Shepard of men.

You will have to be an Avant Garde to bring enhancements and improvements into the world (fruition). We are habitual creatures who become comfortable with what goes on day to day. You can grow accustomed to things that dulls your senses. These behaviors initially will be damaging and degrading until after a while your senses can normalize it.

Just like Stockholm syndrome, where a person being abused grows accustomed to the abuser so much so that they cannot see life without them. This is an extreme example of someone becoming accustomed to something that is terrible (for more on Stockholm Syndrome see chapter 44).

CHAPTER EIGHT:

TO GO WITH THE FLOW

To go with the flow is to be totally taken by external forces while not doing anything to change the course of happenings. (Inertia) Nothing is ever accomplished by being taken over by circumstances while not having any say so in the matter.

I have experienced going with the flow and I have noticed that whatever you want in life is shoved aside to accommodate others and/or society standards. If you want something to happen in life you have to assert your will. Never let others assert their will upon you.

Many people are not used to change. But a great trait to have in life is adaptability. To be adaptable is to be able to change with the circumstances. This is not to change every aspect about yourself but only what is necessary. You may not like this change, but this is where authenticity comes into play.

Many people are just go with the flow people. They never have any say on what trends or behaviors will be next. But to be a trend setter opposes going with the flow. A good practice for improving your life is daily reflection.

Imagine you are on your death bed with less than twenty- four hours until your final breath is upon you.

These are usually the moments humans are forced to reflect on their lives. What regrets would you have about the present time your living in? What accomplishments would you have that out lives your life and potentially make you immortal? What would you have done differently?

For me personally I have been a "nice guy" my entire life thus far. Being a "nice guy" has many benefits but it makes you a push over for individuals who seek to take advantage of easy going, easy to forgive individuals. This is an example of reflection. To reflect on your actions, behaviors and effects of your behaviors is what makes you superior.

Many people are too cowardice to make any beneficial changes in their own lives. Too many run from hardship that confronts them. Instead of becoming an outcast, weak people would rather cave in and conform, instead of becoming the best they can be by setting themselves apart.

Conformity shall be the enemy. Anyone who does conform shall be the enemy as well. We live in a world where it is celebrated to wear uniforms and conformity is the norm. Where most people only see the daises, roses and sunshine; non-conformist see the hell like environment that surrounds us all. And we decide to do something about it instead of becoming overtaken by external pressures. This type of thinking is revolutionary.

Historians tend to believe Jesus, most influential man in modern history, was a peace-loving person who did not concern himself with the happenings of the world. But this previous sentence is not the whole truth. Jesus went to war with Rome and the Pharisees (who were religious pawns for the Roman Government). Maybe this warfare was more spiritual than physical war, but this conflict still had physical elements of war such as bloodshed and a revolution.

But essentially Jesus never went with the flow. He was a non-conformist. He surely did not go with the flow nor was he ever a passivist like Ghandi and Dr. Martin Luther King (who chose "civil disobedience" and passivism to combat the system). To quote Jesus from The New Testament in Luke 22:36, when Jesus had the premonition that he would be killed soon, he informed his follower's "*But now If you have a purse, take it, and also a bag; and if you don't have a sword, sell your cloak and buy one*". This is one quote of many that tends to be ignored by many. This is equivalent to saying trade your clothing for a gun in modern terms. This is the true Jesus Christ.

We live in a paradoxical world where good can be considered evil and evil can be considered good. So, a vice could transform into a virtue just like a virtue could turn into a vice. For instance, patience is a very well-known virtue. This would subsequently make impatience a vice. But to be patient or tolerant to terrible behaviors or actions should never be acceptable. This specific situation is where the vice of impatience is to be considered a virtue. Great people are/should be walking contradictions in this world of paradox.

I am not coming from a utopian point of view. This may be considered idealistic, but these ideas could be exactly what the world is missing. This is how to combat the injustices of colonialism, capitalism and inequality to just name a few. It would never become better if we just go with the flow and wait for someone else to better our world. Let us not forget that this is our world. We set what is acceptable by what we allow.

Let us great thinking individuals become like fire. Let our ideas spread like fire and anyone without these ideals be burned by even attempting to grasp these ideas. This is for the superior humans of the world.

Conformity shall be the enemy and any agents of conformity, let us go to war with our ideas. Vice and virtue start with self-examination and self-reflection. Once we put these activities into our daily practices, then we shall receive the fruits of our labor. First, start by planting the seeds, determining the nature of the roots of the tree that will flourish.

CHAPTER NINE:

PASSION

Passion is to be considered a virtue but when we are passionate about the wrong things it becomes a vice. This is when we have to redeem our passion and refocus it on more effective things. Vices are to be considered aspects of us that needs refocusing. Therefore, vice and virtue should not be considered good or bad. To forgive easy might be considered a virtue but this should be honed to forgive those things that are absolutely essential for our development. Some things should never be forgiven, forgotten or overlooked.

CHAPTER TEN:

THE PATH

The path to perfecting yourself is a lonely one in nature. No one will be able to accompany you. To seek companionship is a wasteful endeavor. You may never be fully understood, if so, only by a select few. There may be times when you feel the need to act but it is best do nothing that you feel doubt about. Only confidently do the things you know is right for yourself.

You may become an aimless wanderer. Your propensities are guided by unseen forces. These unseen forces have more power than we are aware of. The path to greatness is surely lonely meant for the select few. The work can only be done by yourself solely. It is best to seek discomfort so you can learn to rely on your endurance and will power only.

Relationships with friends, family and everyone else will be lost unless they have the necessary understanding. Never seek understanding because dreams happen to you and for you. To seek other interpretations is a wasteful endeavor indeed. To be alone does not mean you have to be lonely. To be lonely means your living out of lack. You should realize you have everything you need for the journey. The less baggage you have the better it is for the journey.

CHAPTER ELEVEN:

MIND OVER MATTER

Strengthen your mind to withstand any tribulations and/or turbulations. To your mind you have many things available to you. Having many things available to your mind offers you the ability to deteriorate your mind or construct it with anything that is available to you. Some of the things to strengthen your mind are mainly practices that you must implement into your daily routine.

One of the most important tools we have is solitude. Solitude is a practice that consists of spending time away from external influences. Meditative practices are key to not losing your mind during very quiet times of solitude.

Meditation will give you solace during stressful times. During times of solitude it is best to strengthen your mind by developing your mind (example gaining knowledge) as a daily routine. You can gain knowledge through various ways. But you should become acquainted with all forms of studies like astronomy, philosophy, theosophy, psychology, economy, metaphysics, religion, mythology, astrology, classic literature, phonology, linguistics etc. This will aid you in becoming greater on your path every day.

But greatness comes at a price and this price is called sacrifice. Greatness only comes to those willing to journey alone. If not now than when. There is no better time to better yourself then the present moment.

CHAPTER TWELVE:

PROCRASTINATION

Procrastination is the enemy to our development. Let us wage a war with procrastination. To wait is to postpone the process of our betterment or greatness. The road to greatness is not an easy task, so it is best that we welcome the uncomfortable moments life has to offer us.

The journey is gruesome, lonesome and tiresome. But it is only meant for some. The moments we do not look forward to are the moments that refine us and build character within us. These improvements are never cosmetic. They are always changes made within us. Meaning some may never notice these improvements unless they were acquainted with who we once were. We can change our outer appearances time and time again but that does not build character. We may garnish our decaying corpses with diamonds, gold, cool tattoos and fancy clothing but this will never amount to a shortcut to greatness. The improvements or change are shown through our character; our words, our thoughts and our actions. These are the only true visible signs to our greatness. These alterations cannot wait. Let us wage war against procrastination and mediocrity as well. An old African proverb is "There is enough room in the sky for all birds to fly" meaning there is room for everything even the mediocre, but only if you do not mind being synonymous with the mediocre that tends to trend. I view mediocre as being synonymous with procrastination so if you wish to escape the herd, embrace the journey now.

CHAPTER THIRTEEN:

QUESTIONS & ANSWERS

Are you willing to live a life being misunderstood? Are you willing to shed blood, sweat and tears to become a "superman"? Will you give up all weaknesses you have been depending on? Will you be able to keep your secrets to yourself? Will you be able to not seek attention? Will you be able to run from hoes instead of chasing them? Can you withstand any criticism? Can you withstand any ridicule? Can you work through stressful times? Can you work through a depressed mind? Will you fold under the pressure? Can you allow your thoughts to live? Will you identify with your thoughts that come and go? Will you learn not to allow your thoughts to control you? Will you embrace that inner spark of God? Will you embrace your individuality? Can you become one with the universe? Will you be able to kill your demons? How will you gather strength during your weakest times?

CHAPTER FOURTEEN:

DISPLEASURES

Life is a series of unfortunate events. Maybe a few surprises along the way. But it is best to sacrifice a part of yourself to benefit the sum total of your being. For me happiness is sacrificed for the price of greatness.

I have given up joy and pleasure, and pain and displeasure has taken its place.

Doing what you love can only happen while confronting things you dislike. Never allow yourself to be overtaken by moments of displeasure. To do what is truly pleasing you must endure unpleasant times. The mind is the source of pain and pleasure. It is best to be mindful of what you can control. You can influence other's thoughts and actions, but to control them outright is not ethical.

I am disgusted with other's behavior at times. I tend to feel neglected and inadequate to society. But I have learned to perceive things as they are and not what I want them to be. Other's actions are ultimately out of my control. I no longer feel the need to change the world into what I like. The best way to change the outside world is to start with in. Your mentality is your tool to bettering everything.

CHAPTER FIFTEEN:

TO CLEAVE (CLINGING)

Please know and take note to never cleave to anyone, anything, anyplace or any situations. All things in life and of life are temporary. Do not cling to life, death or even the afterlife. It is best to enjoy things and people as if we were passersby in the carnival of life. Enjoying things as they come and go. Things that soothe your mind, body, and soul causes pain vice versa.

So, let us not cleave to just getting by, by trying to soothe righteous pain. Let us embrace the pain just as much as the pleasure. But do not cleave to pain or pleasure or any dualities. Not even to life and/or death because when it is time to go it means it is time to let go!

CHAPTER SIXTEEN:

EXPERIENCES

Your experiences are unique to your circumstance. It is probable that there might be a small percentage of people that may have similar experiences. But I think it will be highly unlikely to find someone that correlates to you one hundred percent. So, to seek to be understand is a futile endeavor. I understand that to be misunderstood is not a good feeling. But your circumstances will never match some else's.

To be conscious of everything you do will allow you to become everything you are. When you are mindful of your actions and words you will naturally refine your behavior and character. This is how we transform from mediocre to great.

Life and sleep are continually experienced consecutively. During sleep we experience lucid dreams, where we have complete awareness or consciousness while dreaming. "Lucid living" is to have awareness of all senses while awake. Let us live lucidly. Live a life of meaning. This meaning can only be defined by you. To live a life without meaning is to live an unfulfilled life.

What is meaning? Meaning is substance. Meaning causes movement. Meaning is a life force. Therefore, what gives you life is what is to be considered meaningful. Only you know what invigorates and/or vitalizes your well-being. Do not look to others to define what you are.

CHAPTER SEVENTEEN:

TRADITIONS

We follow patterns of limitations due to comfort and security. There are traditions we destroy and bad traditions we uphold. Time is forcing us to change but something must remain constant during times of evolution. You must choose which traditions to revere and which to destroy.

This decision is usually quite obvious but difficult to come to terms with. This due to our fear of change. We have grown accustomed to mediocrity. So much so that we now believe it to be acceptable. The aspects of our culture we must uphold are all those traditions which enables us to live genuine, remarkable trailblazing lives.

Consequently, we must destroy those aspects of culture which degrades our character. Our disillusioned thoughts and ego driven minds want us to believe we are always right, even during our times of doing wrong. But we need a quality I coined as "emotional maturity" to decipher through childish thoughts and behaviors.

These habits we perform daily are rituals and the success you receive as a result is part magic and part will power. Our attitudes are key. We create by utilizing our will power which transfers to our thoughts and our actions reflect our thoughts. This is the sequence of actions. To be aware of this sequence is to begin to have control and awareness in your life.

What if your traditions were utterly destroyed and continually unable to build any solid foundation? You would then be forced to develop your own set of morals to live by and firmly base a future upon. While we are unfamiliar with our ancestral ways, we are lost until a great way of living is found.

You must will to existence the type of culture you wish to see. However, greatness shall never be a norm, only an exception (for the exceptional). We must define greatness for ourselves and see that as what we aspire to become.

To form tradition, we must acknowledge our instinctual sensations. Friedrich Nietzsche says that our" sensations are ingredients of our will", so we must examine our propensities or urges. Then we must take into account which urges should be considered beneficial and/or detrimental. Ones we must focus on and hone or those which we must destroy.

To know details of our ancestral traditions may be difficult to retrieve. But what we are familiar with are our urges, sensations and intuitive thoughts. These will be our tool to determine our tradition. Subsequently we must purify our entire being (mind, body, and soul) to feel. We must detoxify. You will naturally detect what must be developed and/or what must be destroyed.

CHAPTER EIGHTEEN:

DETERMINATIONS

You must know who has lived a life that is deservedly recognized as one to be upheld. This is a definition of a determination. Whose works were sound and perfectly true for all mankind (which is a signification of an "absolute truth")? We are all aware of

Jesus Christ but are we familiar with his philosophies and daily behaviors?

We must become familiar with the lives of the great heroes of the past and present to gain alignment in becoming the great heroes of the future. These great heroes appear in all walks of life.

Great heroes range from very "Good Samaritans" to high ranking political figures. They all play a vital role in the order of the world. The lower keeps the higher upheld, while the higher sustains the lower. This is an example of a determination. To examine and determine the purpose of anything is to make determinations.

We must dissect the habits, words, struggles, temptations, and over all daily practices of all the great humans from all levels of greatness. What is it about a

"Good Samaritans" behavior that makes them remarkable? Also, what makes a high-ranking political person great?

To this, I would identify the commonality of them taking their time and allocating it towards the space of assisting others. Those that devote their lives and/or livelihoods towards helping others are viewed as fools by some, but I view this type of devotion as an implication of highly developed (great) humans.

I consider this process "Distinguishing who is distinguished". While making determinations, you must remain determined because society turns lions into cowards like the circus. They will take your rings like sonic and bring you down a rung. All those who became tamed lost their name. This is a determination.

CHAPTER NINETEEN:

IDLENESS

I am brave enough to question our sayings and traditions passed down through the times. For instance, the saying "An idle mind is the devil's playground". I pondered upon this phrase for days just as I do with everything that perplexes me. First, I was in agreement with this misguided saying. Until I gained a better understanding on idleness by investigating boredom.

We tend to look at idle behavior as wasting time because we are consumed by an unnaturally busy society. When we participate in systems that schedule our entire lives, we tend to replace our happiness and fulfillment with monetary gain and other futile endeavors.

Ultimately, I have learned that many amazing insights result from an empty, idle, still and unbusy mind. There is only so much to do in our lifetime. You could do everything there is to experience in life. But boredom will creep through the crevasses. This is due to the power in idleness versus the activities of the world.

The world is constantly busy. Everyone seems anxious to get nowhere. The body should stay in motion, but the mind should be still (but the mind and body needs rest and activity respectively). Boredom is essential for the growth process. Boredom is the pocket of air to breathe, think and do whatever YOU deem meaningful. Whether it is a walk in a park (literally) or being absorbed by nature and the profoundness of the different worlds of existence which coexist within one another world harmoniously (like birds, bees, fish, trees and the human anatomies), we can learn to appreciate boredom. I encourage you to try it out. You will only experience different results then what the constant busy world has to offer. You may get your best results yet. So, make sure to allocate time to do nothing.

CHAPTER TWENTY:

HUNGER

Hunger epitomizes the sensations of lack sent to our finite bodies. Hungers source is from perceived lacking, which could cause greed or other qualities if not channeled appropriately. These deficiencies can become infinitely and exponentially magnified if not controlled and rectified. We are required to fuel ourselves with energy by indulging in food, but it is frowned upon to overindulge. Before we eat, we are clear minded more than any other time in the day. But when we overindulge in fatty foods (cholesterol), we clog our blood, stopping proper blood flow from happening. This is due to the fact that the human body produces enough cholesterol for itself to function properly. So, note that any intake of additional fatty substances is already overindulgent. I bring up the chemical cholesterol because it is an example of something your body may perceive to be lacking. But because of our hunger, we fail to recognize our greedy behavioral ways. That is why we must fast occasionally in order to detox ourselves from all the waste we indulge in. However, hunger plays both sides because its aides vice and virtue. This is why I consider hunger to be a neutral quality available to us. Although hunger causes clarity of mind for some rational folks.

It is possible that it could have a perverse effects on some, by causing confusions. These confusions tend to force our weak-willed selves' hand in vice.

CHAPTER TWENTY-ONE:

THE MIND

The mind is the only thing that deserves our absolute devotion. The mind is there for you and always supports you through the good and bad times. I determined that the mind is the only thing that deserves unbridled devotion because it is the only thing that has not left me.

Girlfriends, drugs, food, music are some things I have grown to enjoy, and they all have left me at some point in time. For instance, during times of heart break my love interest would discard me like I was trash (at the time I probably was trash *joke*) but mind was the only thing left and my last line of defense.

Once the mind goes you lose everything meaningful. The mind is neither good nor bad but rather a mirror for your thoughts, actions, and words. I would only categorize aspects of the mind as "good" and /or "bad" based upon thought patterns that either harms or helps the development of the mind.

Mind is the only thing available to offer us true comfort. You may have family, but imagine you grew old while everyone you knew and loved died around you. Then you no longer have family and friends available. Then who or what will be available for continuity? The mind.

Once all else fails us we only have our minds. But if that mind is not supported, strengthened, and utilized properly we could possibly lose our minds and officially lose it all (or maybe all we had to offer). The mind is all. The mind is analogous to the universe. The mind creates everything.

All things that matter are not made of matter. This previous statement means that the thing that holds most importance in reality are usually not made of physical material or matter. We cannot deny the importance of food, clothing, home and shelter, but without the invisible nonmaterial force of love, your house will only be an empty shell or perhaps any empty sleeping capsule. Love is an integral part of life and human development of the mind.

CHAPTER TWENTY-TWO:

STRUGGLE

The struggle of life will aid you as a tool for the development of vice and/or virtue. During times of struggle you may experience hunger, which could push one to fast (virtue) or steal food if not available (vice).

Struggles of life can develop your character and/or damage it. It depends on what we allow to fester in our minds. This is how struggle can be utilized to sharpen one's qualities and/or allowed to damage one's qualities.

If you are able to develop your character, thoughts, actions, and words during chaotic times of struggle and/or perhaps be regularly calm during completely trying turbulent times, you will evolve yourself.   Vice versa, you could possibly degrade yourself by actions which could be considered self-debasement.

The struggle is not going anywhere because ultimately it is a part of natural order. Developments are only made by rigorous hours of struggle. So, struggle has a purpose of refining us and/or degrading us based on our ability to be motivated by struggle and/or depressed by struggle. I hope to have expounded upon the necessity of struggle.

CHAPTER TWENTY-THREE:

POSSESSIVENESS

Possessiveness is a quality that signifies inferiorities stemming from the shadow casted by a person's persona. While performing shadow work, mainly contemplation and studying, I discovered many inferior aspects about myself. Possessiveness is one of the qualities that arose in my mind during my shadow work exercises.

I realized that I have a mind that wants to possess everything it enjoys or gain's pleasure from (Dopamine; see Chapter Forty- Four: Pleasure). For instance, If I see an attractive woman, I say to myself "I want her" or "I got to have her". This type of rhetoric is common amongst men's dialogue. This jargon is possessive in nature.

Possessiveness is an ego centric way of thinking that tricks you into believing you own something, someone or some idea. Freedom accompanies the acknowledgement of your personal inferiorities.

Ownership is never what we think it is. We may have ideas that we birth like children but once these ideas exist, they belong to the universe. Truly a higher power has always been our source.

We humans should consider ourselves conduits, vessels and intermediaries. These are examples of titles that express non-possessiveness and illustrates one of our true purposes. These titles should be worn like crowns because they express our true essence.

Inferiorities arise from what you are unconscious of. If you have a persona around others, you will automatically cast a shadow. This shadow that is produced by our persona has many negative qualities. But ultimately these vices should be looked upon as redeeming qualities just as I have said before.

But In my opinion, we do not possess qualities, rather qualities possess us. The traits we believe to possess, own and/or apart us, are actually things that existed prior to our physical existence. These qualities have a life of their own, with likes and dislikes that they are uniquely attracted to. This attraction usually starts unconsciously, and the results are noticed consciously.

We do not know what causes certain ideas to be drawn to individuals because this happens unconsciously initially. This disproves the illusion of humans being able to possess because it is us who are possessed by characteristics and personality types that are drawn/attracted to us. Ultimately, we are the possessions of thought forms.

CHAPTER TWENTY-FOUR:

ADAPTABILITY

Adaptability is to be changeable according to various situations. I consider being adaptable to be an example of a virtue because it does no damage if practiced properly and its objective is to assist others. When someone is adaptable, they can be put into many situations and find ways to function and thrive in all scenarios. Adaptability is synonymous with changeability.

This changeability can be considered by some as expressing qualities that consist of being wishy washy and/or unoriginal. But with adaptability comes a natural form of compromise. Compromise is not something that is good or bad rather it is something that is a natural course in interactions.

Compromises are forms of negotiations that allows for the formation of a unique relationship based upon rules or determinations made by the two involved entities. You could want to appease and please others so much so that you are willing to change aspects of yourself to appeal to others. This nature of being changeable, to me should be a signification of a highly developed individual and/or simply someone who just wants to be liked by others.

Also, adaptability is a quality of someone who is willing to give up things he may have once believed to be a part of himself in order to become rebirthed as something else. Therefore, adaptability is a virtue which demonstrates the transformative, progressive and highly developed individual's pursuit in serving others anyway needed and/or possible. This quality of being adaptable or changeable should be implications of a whole and complete person who is willing to take a part of himself, discard it and/or alter it beyond all recognition, solely to assist others.

CHAPTER

TWENTY-FIVE:

THE UNCONCSIOUS

\

"The unconscious mind is appeased by sacrifice"
says Carl Jung. The unconscious mind is a part of
ourselves, but it is the part of ourselves we deny we are
and/or the parts of ourselves that we may be unconscious
of. When we have a mask or persona around others, then
we automatically cast a shadow. This shadow is a part of
the unconscious mind. The unconscious mind contains
all those things we are afraid of becoming. This shadow
exists because we have not integrated our inferior
qualities and/or have we come to terms with these
aspects of ourselves. This consequently results in a life
of fear and prejudices because one is afraid of himself
and especially afraid of others that embody those traits
that remain underdeveloped in himself.

This process is called integration or
individuation. This is known to be a journey of unifying

divided aspects of your own psyche. Carl Jung says the result of individuation is always a *"God Image"* because this represents wholeness and a merging of two opposing parts, qualities, functions, aspects and/or ideas.

CHAPTER TWENTY-SIX

THE MASK

Our personas are the masks we wear around other people. This persona creates a pedestal which sits the individual at a high place. This position is threatened by anyone who does not have any respect for the persona of the individual. A mountain of pride is the only thing which upholds this lofty position. Any amount of threats to this pride could be exactly what sets the individual off and/or shatters the individual's mask.

This position is only established by pride, so once this pride is threatened this position could be destroyed. Pride will not allow you to consciously degrade yourself, but pride could possibly hinder growth unconsciously if considered to be vital for survival. Ultimately pride is an example of a quality that is neutral, which could lend itself to positive and/or negative qualities.

Pride becomes dangerous when it blinds someone from seeing reality or things as they are. Pride could act as a mask for deficiencies. Therefore, masks are to be considered twins to pride. Masks are worn to influence the public perception of an individual. Just like pride, the role of the masks or personas is to disguise. We usually do not want to be portrayed as who we truly.

The issue with pride is that we are not as important as we may believe we are. But our prideful reactions cause us to believe that we are the center of the universe. But if we set our pride aside for a second and set our masks aside temporarily, we can examine life in its totality (as it is). We can easily recognize that nature can and/or would get along simply without us. This does not mean that our lives lack any importance. But our lives will be more productive and steadfast if we base our existence upon the laws of nature. Once we equip ourselves with a better way of reacting to everyday situations, it is our duty to change with the times. If we fail to update our outdated programming, we could possibly die.

CHAPTER TWENTY-

SEVEN:

WOMEN

Women are dynamite! Delicate yet dangerous, women are not to be tempered with. Women are creators and/or destroyers. I am thankful to my mother supremely for going through with the birth of me because I have realized that I could not have been. Abortion is ultimately a tool for the destruction. Women are capable of the totality of the universe microscopically.

At times it is frightening to me because some women do not know the extent and/or actualize these powers. The psyche of a man opposes women's mind in a cosmic harmonic order. In my opinion women are naturally more decisive while men are more sentimental. Also, in my opinion the mind of women is naturally more developed than the mind of man.

Women have the ability to uplift the soul of a man and/or stomp on it. I tend to feel overwhelmed with opposing emotions or forces whenever in close proximity of women in general. These feelings are unique to encounters with women. I feel lust and love simultaneously. I recognize this as a divine interaction of feelings.

At times I choose to only observe from a distance, never delving into a full experience with women. Mainly due to fear of the unknown, I remain standoffish for my own good reasons. Seduction is like a suction; it draws me in until I am no more good.

CHAPTER TWENTY-EIGHT:

RIDICULE

Ridicule is only experienced when doing what you want. The trailblazers are the ones who set new footprints on unmarked territory. They are always liable to face ridicule. We may define ridicule as the act of not be being taken seriously. Even sometimes ridicule is shown/expressed through harsh criticism which does not seem constructive.

Sometimes we may be unconscious of the significance of the things that we do and its effect. Ridicule is, could and should be taken as s significant sign, signifying progression of one embarking on a path. This ridicule is to be considered as an external force which intrudes on integral parts of ourselves if allowed or even considered.

When someone is going through a paradigm shift imposed by our tiresome selves, our entire being is shifted, changed and/or developed. This totality consists of our minds, bodies, souls, spirits, thoughts, personalities and the roles we play in this universal play will be enhanced greatly. These changes are threatening to opposing external forces which are fond of our previous selves.

Timidity transforms into courageousness. Then we are able to see the parts of ridicule which is to be considered essential for our greatest good.

Therefore, ridicule is only damaging when one is insecure with parts of themselves. You can be considered a fool or an innovator just by your choice to waiver or conquer.

CHAPTER

TWENTY-NINE:

"The meek shall inherit the earth"

"Blessed are the meek, for they will inherit the earth" Matthew 5:5 is a well-known verse from The New Testament which was designed for impressionable minds (slave morality) versus will and command power (master morality). Slave morality is subjected by good consciousness, rules, commandments, and essentially whatever they are told. Master morality is equipped with the ability to command and will what they want.

Masters are able to act on their desires because they have mastered their minds and achieved essentially becoming creators of their own worlds.

Slaves are looked upon as docile, moldable and obedient which all are synonymous with being "meek". A good slave morality is comparable to a properly programmable computer.

To be meek is to be easily imposed upon. Of course, this is looked at as the ideal mentality for humans who are forced to become slaves. Meek individuals are susceptible to being manipulated, abused and/or confused. An individual who is considered meek has usually been broken into submission.

We were tricked into belief, that the individuals who are blessed and will be receiving the inheritance of earth are those who practice good slave morality, which consists of never questioning authorities like the bible, the preacher and/or the so called "slave master". Who was this so called "authority"? Also why is it considered a blessing to be "meek'? Was this quotation from the New Testament sole purpose to indoctrinate? Or are their actual blessings which results from being meek?

To be meek is to be tame, submissive and spiritless. These qualities are descriptions usually utilized by anyone describing a domesticated animal. But as humans, we are endowed with the ability to think, comprehend and respond appropriately. Humans are able to know of the monstrosities committed against ourselves.

More synonyms of "meek" describes its wickedness in nature. For instance, indulgent expresses the tendency to be lenient and/or overly generous. Also, the quality of being meek refers to being patient through long suffering. "Blessed are the meek, for they will inherit the earth" is a false promise that is meant to indoctrinate and/or essentially brainwash.

Based on the definition of inheritance, for me to inherit something, someone would have to die first. The only way to assure that meekness truly results in being blessed and gaining earth as an inheritance, I would have to live my life being submissive which is the opposite of dominant. But I know to become meek, I would be forced to suppress however I truly felt. If I felt anyway opposed from being docile, domesticated and compliant I would have been considered to be blasphemous and/or punished. Maybe the blessings of being meek and its inheritance of earth are gained through the death of your true self and/or your primary state (primal state).

CHAPTER THIRTY:

BAD VERSUS EVIL

We tend to view bad as lacking goodness, but evil is a higher form of badness. Evil only differs from bad because it is condemnable. Evil behaviors versus bad behaviors differ due to its magnitude of effects. Bad is tolerable while evil is not. Evil can be utilized as a fear mechanism, while badness can be viewed as an immature level of seeking one's desires.

Evil should then be considered as sophisticated in comparison to bad which usually feeds on inferiorities. Also bad is subjective, while evil is objective. For example, this can be noticed by any doctrine created which were to be considered as foundations (like constitutions, ten commandments etc.) for whole countries and whole individuals alike. The evils are always objective.

While if we understand art, we would know that no art can be considered solely good or bad. This is an example of why bad is subjective. A self-proclaimed bad quality could be viewed as something good by someone else.

CHAPTER THIRTY-ONE:

PLASTICITY

Plasticity is an idea I came across while reading a book called "The Neuroscience Bible". A man who had a serious brain injury, was studied after the incident. He had damaged parts of his frontal lobe. He developed a personality change due to his injury, going from once calm and easy to work with; to irritable and unsettled. But he was studied over time and scientist realized he had made unusual bounce back developments to his original personality.

This showed that parts of his brain matter damaged from the injury regenerated naturally. This scientific development coined the term "plasticity".

A man who had lost parts of his brain matter connected and in charge of personality and emotions was able to help in the discovery of previously unknown abilities of the brain.

This incident helped in developing a map of the brain and its purposes according to location. Plasticity shows us how a perceived negative event led to the discovery of new information which was unavailable prior. This beautifully terrible injury sheds light upon darkness of the mind and helped in the development of understanding ourself.

CHAPTER THIRTY-TWO: *INFERIORITIES*

Inferiorities are products of our unconscious mind. Our fallacies that we are unaware of rises to the surface as anger, jealousy and/or many other detrimental qualities. Our weaknesses can take a life of their own if not recognized and controlled.

We can identify inferiorities as uncomfortable feelings that arise during quiet times. These inferiorities are created through self-perceived lack. These inferiorities, which are perceived as a lacking a particular quality, will then be highlighted in others.

These behaviors will result in thoughts of jealousy and/or envy because someone has what the individual thinks they lack.

These inferiorities are to be looked at as empty pockets of potential, or a void that must be consciously understood, examined, and developed. The source of inferiorities is the unconscious mind. Acknowledge your inferiorities to become whole. Abundance is a cure for inferiorities. What do you have in abundance?

CHAPTER THIRTY-

THREE:

VICTORIES

Victories are our significations of our greatness but never meant to be dwelt upon. If we stand upon our victories, we will be as high as mountains. But our losses will be terrible pitfalls that go unappreciated. We are capable of creating amazing feats.

Victories will drive us to duplicate previous endeavors to receive praise and/or feel accomplished. Victories then make us stagnant in our potential.

Failure comes from attempting new things and embarking on a venture and/or adventure. There is a beauty in failure that tends to go unappreciated when we are consumed by becoming the victor. Victories can be seen as significations of greatness and/or signs of an empty life.

CHAPTER THIRTY-

FOUR:

ARBITRARY

An arbitrary lifestyle is what I have recently

developed against external pressures (forces) like status

quo, laws, streets rules etc. I define arbitrary as living by one's own accord, moving on a whim and essentially doing whatever you feel at any moment without restrictions of systems and reasoning.

I have developed my own rituals apart from the chaotic, robotic, normalized and unfulfilling rollercoasters of joys and sorrows.

This arbitrariness has given me my own entire world where I am the ultimate controller of space and ultimate utilizer of time.

This world may be defined as a division from what some may consider reality. Most of my days are spent writing, reading, contemplating and fighting demons. These demons or unconscious inferiorities arise during quiet times sometimes. Perhaps they just seek acknowledgement. I use arbitrariness as a technique.

Ultimately, arbitrary is to do what you instinctually feel at any given moment.

The only exceptions are to be determined by yourself of what you can and cannot do. This is one of the vital themes of this book. The root of arbitrary is from Latin arbiter meaning "Judge or Supreme ruler".

CHAPTER THIRTY-FIVE:

TENSION

Tension is the result of two opposing forces in engagement. Tension is a law of nature that can be view from the microscopic world and from the cosmos. In nature, tension is not viewed as a hinderance, instead it is a normal part of the universal interactions.

Study nature and you will see the divine nature all around you. Tension is a space between dualities that connects and simultaneously opposes forces from direct contact. This space can be differences between understanding but ultimately it is a difference between dualities. Tension has its purpose. To gain a full understanding of a thing, we must observe things as they are and not abnormally.

I have observed that tension can be as a cushion or a protective layer for integral parts. Websters standard dictionary defines tension as "the act of stretching, or the condition of being stretched; mental strain, or anxiety. Also, a device on a machine that regulates stress.

My definition seems more cosmological and metaphysical, but I see similarities in both definitions. First, Websters definition expresses tension as stretching, similarly to my definition of tension being the result of two opposing forces in engagement. Secondly, Webster's definition describes "tension as stress, mental strain and/or anxiety". This is a more specific way of describing an observed effect between two opposing forces.

Now I would dare to describe tension as being divine because it happens as an instinctual force which we are usually unconsciously apart of. In my opinion a women's soft exterior and hard interior (decisiveness) versus man's rough exterior and soft interior (sentimentality) sets the way for a divine course of tension.

CHAPTER

THIRTY-SIX:

DECEPTION

Deceptive ways, deception pays. Honesty is a virtue, but it could become potentially harmful if mishandled and overused. In society we force ourselves to have personas when around others. These personas are mask that are habitual forms of deception we all take part in. Pure honesty can be damaging at times.

Your genuine feelings towards something may be considered as cutthroat and could potentially hurt feelings and self-esteems by being completely honest. You could potentially hurt a child by informing them of all the ways of people. There are many levels to deception, and everything must be done with balance.

Truth and honesty are needed just as much as deception and lies. This does not mean that each thought, action and/or statement should rotate between deceptive and/or truthful in nature.

Sometimes it is valid to feel no way. But I am basically saying we should not live lives with too much credence or emphasis on being honest and/or deceptive, there must be a balance. We must determine when it is virtuous to lie and damaging to tell the truth.

CHAPTER THIRTY-SEVEN:

REFLECTION

Reflection is to go within your mind and essentially move time by thinking about events.

Reflection is a tool that allows us to gain hindsight, insight, and perhaps foresight about life experiences. Reflection is different from regretting because you take the perspective of an observer instead of identifying as your past self.

Too much reflection could be detrimental to progression. If you spend too much time in reflection mode, you find yourself harboring on the past and/or present. Then you will be a body in the present but someone with their mind stuck in the past and/or future. I do not know what it would be like to not reflect because we are creations endowed with intellect and the ability to think, comprehend and reflect as natural processes of the human mind.

I would like to guess that a human without the ability to reflect would be someone who constantly lived in the moment. This person would not have the ability to remember past mistakes or errors. Subsequently this individual who lacked the ability to reflect would escape the constant entanglement of dread and/or stress. Reflection is a natural part of our make-up unconsciously. But if we are conscious of our times of reflection, we will then be able to manage the amount of time and energy we will give to reflect.

To conclude, reflection has many definitions besides giving something serious thought. One of these definitions I would like to discuss now is something being thrown back by something else while not allowing anything to be absorbed. This definition is a physical example of the mind deflecting something while not allowing anything in while in reflection mode.

CHAPTER THRITY

EIGHT:

LOSS

Loss is to experience the death of someone, an idea and/or an object. This loss (death) is either figurative and/or literal. When you experience loss, you lose an integral part of your world which results in you potentially becoming lost. When you experience what it means to lose something dear to you, you experience every inferior emotion there is to feel. It is as if waves of emotions takes you over unceasingly with turbulent motion (emotion).

Loss only comes from connectivity, consistency and continuity. When we feel connected to something or someone we feel as they feel. So, with the death of an object, when connectivity is involved, you will always feel a detrimental loss. Consistency is a trait that has great qualities and aspects that may set you back, so let's consider consistency as a neutral quality.

Consistency is a product of our habitual nature. But what we are unconsciously doing consistently could be damaging. But if we become aware of our unconscious habitual behaviors, we will be able to concisely alter our course. If we re-examine ourselves constantly, I know this results in developments.

Continuity is a process of continuous order. This perceived reality (continuity) is intact for the moment so there is continuity. But once a loss takes affect there is a break in this continuity. If our connectivity, consistency and continuity is solely deemed by external forces, we will constantly experience loss in continuity and feel unconnected from something actual.

CHAPTER THIRTY-NINE

SENSITIVITY

Sensitivity is to be easily stimulated whether via mind, body and soul (mentally, physically and/or spirituality). Sensitivity is a part of our instinctual nature as a mechanism against the external world.

Sensitivity allows us the opportunity to avoid incoming danger. Our senses speak to us in various ways. Our physical bodily senses are aroused or stimulated by smell, taste, touch, hearing, and sight.

Our mental sensitivity is also feed by these same sensations stated in the previous sentence. Our spiritual sensitivity could become dull and unnoticeable. Or if developed could give one psychic ability. Sensitivity is known by many common phrases. For instance, when someone says "they are having a gut feeling" this is a signification of incoming potential dangers.

As I have explained, sensitivity is an innate part of our being. But if not tamed and disciplined, we open the risk of becoming overly sensitive or overly caring. Sensitivity can be raised to such a level that an individual can be able to feel the feelings of others without words having to be spoken. This could be very damaging to morale because it will see that you will have to take on all burdens of the world.

Let's not allow sensitivity to run wild, we must control what and how we feel at all times consciously.

CHAPTER FORTY:

ANGER

Anger is a deep and intense emotion that is like a low oven pilot light always lit within us. Anger is something in our life that rarely subsides. Rather it is calmed and attended too. Something may happen in your life which ignites this anger within. Ultimately anger from within must be released momentarily in order to properly, think, function and/or live. Anger causes a person to have tunnel vision on what it is that angered or vexed them. Blinders caused from anger will block everything but what made you angry.

This can be utilized properly by identifying what makes you angry and deciding whether or not this thing that made us upset is actually worth our energy. Therefore, we must prioritize our anger, similarly how we must prioritize aspects of life we deem important in life generally.

Once anger has seized us, we become motivated to reverse this displeasure into something we can control or be pleased with. Therefore, anger is an emotion which highlights things we must focus on. There are examples of anger that is unjustifiable and vice versa. I define an unjustified anger as something that upsets you, but ultimately it being out of your control. Justified anger should be considered as aspects of yourself that makes you upset but must be focused on because it bothers us, and ultimately it is in our control.

CHAPTER

FORTY-ONE:

HAPPINESS

Happiness is the embodiment of the feeling of completion and wholeness. I consider happiness a fleeing feeling that gives us great pleasure. Happiness can be obtained but we must understand the parts of ourselves that should be considered constant and forever unchanging.

Happiness is caused by fixing and making things better. This fixing for happiness is a fixed or unchanging part of existence which causes us to always attempt to identify problems to make better and/or spread happiness. But as they say it is not about the destination (happiness), it is about the journey (constant unchanging fixed position of fixing).

Most people set on their journey destined to reach happiness. But all the while they fail to recognize the work (cause of the happiness) as what is truly meaningful and substantial. The work is constant, and happiness is fleeing.

CHAPTER

FORTY-TWO:

SADNESS

Sadness or depression arises from dependency. Anything that displeases someone should be considered as a vital part of their reality, usually being pointed out by someone and/or something else which is signified by their sadness. We must be observant to know when specific emotions arise.

Emotions must be redefined as signals from our unconscious mind that wants us to recognize what we should improve and ways to improve it.

Subsequently, sadness has a reverse process in comparison to the process of happiness. With happiness we must complete something first in order to be pleased. While with sadness the feeling comes first then the work follows once we determine what it is that makes us sad.

Sadness and happiness are polar opposites. But the substance of which makes up sadness and happiness is a fleeing feeling. Another commonality between happiness and sadness is the work and/or fixing, which must be considered as a constant part of the processes in life. This results in the individual making themselves happy and/or identifying what makes them sad.

CHAPTER FORTY-THREE:

PAST/PRESENT/FUTURE

PAST

The past has passed. The past is a part of reality that once was but is now no longer. When we study the past, we are able to learn from the greatest and/or worst of times. It gives us the ability to know where we went wrong in the past and where did we leave off in terms of developments. No present achievements could be made without the achievements of the past. Acknowledgement of our past affairs would aid us greatly, only if we know how to utilize our past properly.

Our downfalls are sometimes caused by not observing and learning form the past in a more efficient way. People try to identify with cultures, ideas and/or people that no longer exist. These past cultures, ideas and/or people once were, but now they are no longer. Meaning a lot of these things made sense in the past but could potentially be a part of an outdated system.

Let us not give life to something that is deservedly dead. This is preventable by gathering an unfiltered and unbiased information about the past. We must determine aspects of the past that were beneficial and/or damaging. Some stuff we must let go and/or some stuff we must hold on to

PRESENT

Your presence is a present. Present represents the moment of now. The present is constant and the only actual reality. Living in the moment causes you to become an ultimate utilizer of time. Living in the moment has its magic that I hope to capture in this chapter. When I mention time in regard to present, I would like to discuss seconds now.

A second is a unit of time and an enemy of the present. When you wait seconds you naturally second guess yourself. Now instead of doing things now, seconds take affect causing you to second guess yourself. This results in also losing the intensity that was present initially, then to become watered down remnants of what was missed in the moment.

FUTURE

I view the future as the product of the present. The future does not exist unless our presence is forever present. Meaning the role of the present moment, or now, constantly gives new life to the future. For instance, if presently we do not inform kids that they are the future, they may never be aware. Let us enlighten our children of what the past means to the present and how the present is the controller of the future.

Whatever we focus on in the present becomes a present (gift) to the future. To allow your presence of attention to be centered upon the moment of now, you have influence on the future based upon our presence in the present (the now). Future events should not be pushed off to be completed later. Instead we must fulfill the future now by not waiting seconds or second guessing ourselves.

CHAPTER FORTY-FOUR:

STOCKHOLM SYNDROME (THE ROMANTICIZATION OF THE DEVIL)

Why is it that we entertain lies rather than embrace the truth? Lies are upheld solely by our inability to see the benefit in the truth. We go along with lies for self-preservation and security purposes. Lies can give us a sense of security from the truth which tends to deliver harsh blows. We can live a lie for an entire lifetime.

Then encountering the truth causes a shock to our entire system.

We are habitual creatures who are against changes and new ways of doing things. To determine lies in comparison to truths, take note that deception is usually well thought-out with levels of complexities. While the truth tends to be short, sweet and simple. Our habitual behaviors cause us to familiarize ourselves with "convenient truths". Unknowingly we fall into feeling dumbfounded because we have taken on other's beliefs and/or lifestyles, then considered them to be our own truths.

Stockholm syndrome is defined as an abnormal relationship developed between a victim being abused and their abuser. This bond between victim and abuser is created by time spent in intimacy. Stockholm syndrome equates to "The Romanticization of the Devil. Devils (or the evils) take various forms.

Some of these formations are expressed in spiritual, metaphysical, theoretical and/or anthropomorphic configurations. "The Devil" can be an abuser in a domestic abusive relationship or a parasite in the form of a worm which enters the body and releases toxicities. Imagine becoming bonded, acquainted and/or fond of a parasite leeching from you. This example of a relationship between host and parasite is an analogy for Stockholm syndrome and/or "the romanticization of the devil"

This is a classic example of what I would call "the confusion of vices and virtues" which results in a person's inability to make proper discernment for themselves.

CHAPTER

FORTY–FIVE:

UNCONDITIONAL LOVE

Unconditional love is the solution to many obstacles. Unconditional Love frees us from having to choose sides. This form of love is demonstrated when you love yourself in all forms ranging from lowly to high in position. Despite not liking certain particularities of individuals, remembering that inner spark of God within each and every living thing allows you the opportunity to love unconditionally. This remembrance will lead you to becoming aware of others as an extension of yourself, by identifying that spark of God as the common thread weaved between all life forms. Remember we were all once pure, but we became corrupted somewhere along the way.

I describe God as a verb. To me God is the will to do. Love is the emotion of God. Therefore, for us to practice unconditional love, consequently we are practicing being God-like. Each aspect plays specific purposes and are essential for perfect divine order.

Our human perception is not equipped to comprehend terrible things, occurrences and/or people serving a heavenly purpose. We must recognize the barrier between humans attempting to understand divine order as being out of our range of intellect. But what we can understand is the concept of unconditional love. To love all things all the time is unconditional love.

To love my underdeveloped form just as much as my developed self is unconditional love. We must understand that all forms of life play an essential role in enhancements.

The good and the bad are interchangeable based on experiences perceived. You are not the "good" or "bad" you, rather you are the spectator. The spectator observes the "good" and/or "bad' from within but does not identify as neither.

CHAPTER

FORTY-SIX:

PLEASURE

Pleasure comes from receiving delight from sense experiences (a chemical compound called dopamine). From my experiences I have noticed various sources of pleasure that affects the human mind. Sexual intercourse is one route to experiencing high forms of pleasure which typically does not last long. Afterward it is normal to feel drained by sexual intercourse. This form of pleasure seems to be one of many forms of pleasure that has a draining effect.

Sex consumes physical and/or libido energy then it potentially leaves the participant weaker than before. There are other forms of pleasure that rejoices one's "aura" or energetic field. For instance, when I read books that contain certain information that enlightens me on many topics, I was unaware before, I tend to feel strengthened and/or refreshened. This form of pleasure revitalizes your energy instead of depleting it.

Pleasure that energizes your body and mind differs from that which takes away. Pleasure is the pursuit of all. But to pursue a pleasure which consumes energy instead of recharging us, leaves us in a docile

state, which potentially extinguishes our drive to do.

Made in the USA
Middletown, DE
28 February 2023

25703439R00077